To every family member and friend that helped me through the past two years. Thank you.

INTO THE ETHER
POETRY AND PROSE

Into the Ether Poetry and Prose

Rebecca J Chamberlain

publisher logo

1

Ignorance is Bliss

Haiku 1

Vanilla chai tea
Cold Sunday morning outside
Walk around the park

Over a Year

I'm angry the sun can make you warm
When my hands are always cold
And I'm angry death will always have you
After we have grown old
I'm sad that leaving me was easy
Like I never meant anything to you
And I'm sad you found the worst in me
When you knew me through and through
But I'm happy
I'm happy you've returned to me
You came back safe and sound
And I'm happy you're yourself again
My feelings are profound
I'm happy for all the days we have
No matter what the weather
And I'm happy for every living moment
That we can spend together

Before Catastrophe

At the end of the day I feel very mean
I'm so tired from working all day
I walk and I talk and I cook and I clean
But only ten minutes passed away

You Left

Your skin was brown and your hair was black
You were handsome and sharp as a tack
You left one day
And didn't say
When you would ever come back

Again

I didn't feel loved by you today
For me
It was a week from hell
Busy
And everything wrong happening all at once
We bickered from the moment you got home
You didn't sweep
Or do the dishes last night
There's a heat wave
A bug infestation
Work was hectic
Failed manifestations
And for you
I would have watched your favorite show
Or cooked your favorite meal
But for me
You fell asleep on the couch
Again

Wifey

I go to work to do my job
Then I come home and do my job
And the only time I have for me
Is the 30 minutes before I'm asleep
Or those two minutes when I go pee
And in that time
That is mine
I shut my eyes to calm my mind
But I need to go grocery shopping
And the laundry isn't done
And I need to vacuum
And go for a run
This is just my life at 24
Barely married and with no kids
I'm exhausted, nearly dead
And in this house
I make more money than my spouse
So I have to bring home the bread
But I need to go grocery shopping
Why is everything never stopping
Dare I snap or say I'm stressed
Time to vacuum
I need to get dressed
But the laundry isn't done

I'm having so much fun
Help? I could ask
But you know men with small tasks
I can't wait until next week!
This is just the life
Of being a wife
It's 11 PM now
I'm not going for a run

June 29th Entry

This past weekend we all went to the planetarium in Boston as a late Mother's Day/Father's Day gift. I love planetarium shows - this one was on the whole universe. At one point in the show, it zoomed out to everything we as a society can see/know about space. Past trillions of things, tons of planets and stars and as it zoomed out, it was just one big ball of bright light. Could this be the "light" everyone describes when dying? Are we just becoming one with the universe? It was so lovely I teared up. The others said it made them realize how small they are compared to everything. It made me feel lucky. Miraculous. Grateful. Our chances of being here are already slim but this just made me realize just how much more slim the chance really is. Wow. I feel amazing. I have been counting my blessings every day. I am thankful I can walk and talk and know things. Screw material items. I don't feel small, I feel extraordinary. Like a happy bit of star dust who will become star dust again in 80 years.

Women

One day I'll watch you do it for our kids
And I know I'll feel upset
Because why do moms, daughters, and women
Always get the shit end of the stick

July 6th Entry

Today, I ate a creamy avocado. It's 85 degrees and not raining finally. Also, a good hair day. I love life's little reminders that it won't always suck. Also, I ate chocolate today.

7|6|83

Today I ate a creamy avocado.
It's 85 degrees and not
raining finally. Also a good
hair day. I love life's little
reminders that it won't always
suck. Also I ate chocolate today.

Original Entry

My Whole Body

I have legs that walk
And feet that dance
Arms that hug
And hands that grab
Ears that listen
Eyes that view
A voice that cries
Out for you
A mind full of memories
And a heart full of pain
But no love for you
Runs through these veins

Dear Becky

A friend of a friend
Who's now my own friend
It's brown
It's pink
Dry heaving in a sink
Becky is pregnant
I think I've lost one again
Happy Birthday Becky
I envy my friend
It's too early in the season
To start feeling depressed
Same fights with my man
About how he's obsessed
I feel suicidal
Now I'm stressed
Because it's been years
Going 90 on the highway
Trying to focus through tears
And Becky tells me
She loved her gift
Which was just my presence
Becky doesn't know
That on that day
She saved my life

How pathetic to say I'm
Just an overwhelmed wife

Teacher

I'm so tired
Of teaching men
Basic life lessons
Like
How to save money
Or
That the phrase
If you want to
Isn't an invitation
I won't teach you how to
Cook
Clean
Work
Save
Spend
And especially
Not how to love me

2

Midi

The Birds

I often wonder why
Birds don't fly
Wherever they want
They could go anywhere in the world
Yet they stay in one general area
Is it because they have a sense of home?
Is it because they have family groups
They want to stay close to?
Do they think the same of me?
I am a human
With free will
Could I not go wherever I want?
Europe, North America, South East Asia
Yet I too stay in one general area
Near my home
Near my family
Am I so alike as the bird?
What does he wonder of me
I should just admire him
And enjoy his song
And enjoy my life
However long

I Thought The Grim
Was My Friend

A long time ago
There was a voice
That screamed in my head
When I was depressed
You could just die
You'll feel better when you are dead

So a couple of times
I gave it a shot
Whenever things got bad
It never worked
And so I just
Continued on being sad

Years go by
And I'm better now
Except for when people cry
Or when they tell me
That I've hurt them
And I don't know the reason why

I get this feeling

Of crashing waves
Deep within my chest
A doom filled storm
In my mind
When I've been trying my best

My loved ones are angry
I've done it again
And I think that the voice has gone
Until it whispers
You could just die
I am just the reaper's pawn

Sunny

I like to walk in the sun
On bright days it's really fun
Until I burn
On my heel I turn
And after 5 minutes I'm done

To Dance

I want love and I want to be known. I want someone to dance with me.

Time for Ballet

Left hand on the bar
First position
Plié, relevé, plié and stretch
Second position
Plié, relevé, plié and stretch
Fifth position
Plié, relevé, plié and stretch
Plié sous-sus
Plié, stretch, and finish
Turn, right hand on the bar
Left side

Tendus
32 relevés in first
8 rond de jambes en dehors and en dedans
8 dégagés en croix
16 pas de bourrées
Fondus
Développés
8 frappés en croix

STRETCH!

16 sautés in first

Chaine turns
Piqué turns
Tombé, pas de bourrée, glissade, saut de chat

Curtsy to your teacher

I'm tired

Divine

Nighttime thinking
Were my day time worries
Stressful dreaming
Not feeling well rested
Prophecies and omens
I'm being tested
Making life's decisions
Based in slumber
But to the Gods
I'm just a number
I stroll through life
Looking for a sign
Just to be reminded
My existence is divine

Water & Air

I want to flow
Like water
Like a river
Like a stream
I want to be free
Like air
Like a cloud
Like a dream

At the Beach

Shells in the sand
The world in my hand
The tide brings the foam out to
sea

Gray is the sky
The waves are too high
Life has begun to drown me

First Draft of At the Beach

At the Beach

Shells in the sand
The world in my hand
The tide brings the foam out to sea

Gray is the sky
The waves are too high
Life has begun to drown me

January 3rd

The waves have washed over me
Leaving bits and pieces
Grains of sand
Small shells
Sea glass
I'm free
I'm pure
I'm clean

Horrors

I am resilient strong and persistent
I've seen the terrors that life can be
I've stared down the long barrel of its gun
The horrors should be horrified of me

Like Mine

With a life like mine, the poetry comes easy
Really truly
The poetry comes too easy
It practically writes itself

Greek Gods

As Pygmalion created Galatea
Mold me into what you want me to be
Your lover, your friend
Your other, your wife
Your ivory statue who's now come to life

Medicine

When life gets so bad
I sleep away the pain
But in my dreams, there's still no escape
Nightmares plague me
And I don't feel sane
Avoidance and slumber don't medicate

3

Family & Friends

Sister

If nothing rhymes with orange
Then despair rhymes with mister
Warmth rhymes with family
And love rhymes with sister

If nothing rhymes with orange
Then despair rhymes with mist
Warmth rhymes with family
And love rhymes with siste

Becca

Amelia Brown is in Town

She buys the new fashions
And follows the trends
She lives her life very nobly
But when she was young
And taller than her friends
She resembled the Jungle Book's Mowgli

She's smart as a whip
More gorgeous than a God
But boy can that girl snore
She says funny things
Though she can be odd
And her knee is always so sore!

I love her dearly
More than my own life
I do not tell her enough
I hope I have not
Caused her any strife
Because sometimes my love is tough

So tell me a joke
And snore in my ear
I love you with much intensities
The love of sisters
You should not fear
It's just the bear necessities

She's Lovely

Sometimes my sister
Is a little bit mean
But I can't be angry
Cause she learned it from me

Emma

My Emma is a gem-a
Sweeter than you or them-a
The poem to my prose
The stem to my rose
And she is the crème de la crème-a

A Friend

I think about how I can ever repay my friends for being there for me through the hardest time of my life. For listening to me ruminate about the same situation 100 times. None of them ever told me to stop or that I was annoying. They would listen and help me analyze. They still spent time with me when I moped and loved me when I felt like I was insane with jealousy and rage. They supported every decision I made. I was never humiliated or made to feel like a burden. How do you repay a friend for that? I think if it were to happen to them and they came to me for solace, what would I do? The same thing. Listen to them, support them, love them. And if they were ever to ask how they could repay me I would look at them puzzled. Repay me for what? This is the very essence of what being a friend is. You can repay me only by continuing to be one.

The Family Dynamic

My mother and my sister fight all the time. They have such similar personalities that they butt heads frequently. My mother, however, favors my sister ever so slightly over me. They are stubborn and hide their emotions so when they fight they would never make it seem like they care about each other. Always nonchalant, the fights never "bothering" them. This fuels my sister's anger while making my mom think my sister hates her. I watch as an outsider and beg them to open up a little. I tell my mom to talk about her feelings. I tell my sister to appreciate the little things our mom does before it's too late. My sister knows I love her unconditionally. I try to express how grateful I am to my mom; I pour the love on thick and earnestly, so she knows she's not hated. But why does it matter coming from the kid who doesn't matter in the first place.

My Mum

My mother has gentle hands
And the strength of a warrior
I hope she knows how sorry I am
For all the times I used to worry her

My mom's the smartest woman I know
And she's an advocate for justice
If she can only remember one thing
I love her truly, let it be just this

My mum, the scientist
The housekeeper, the chef
She gives the best hugs
She's just overall the best

Statistics

Good fathers are rare
For mine I am grateful
Even after puberty
He never turned hateful

He didn't come from much
But made his way in this world
He'd do anything for his wife
And his two little girls

I would scream it from roof tops
Put posters up in town
Tell the whole population
He's the greatest dad around

My Dad

My Dad's funny
My Dad's kind
My Dad never
Changes his mind

So last year
When he called me vain
Do you think today
He feels the same

I went to school
I read books
I never focused
Just on looks

At my job
I did shine
Do you think Dad
Changed his mind

Now I make
A chunk of change
Do you think Dad

Still feels the same

Cemetery

Do you think the departed
Sit upon where they're buried
Do they use their stones
As a tray for treats and tea
Do you think they stroll among us
Do you think they see us coming
Does gramma give a kiss to me?

Immigrants

Street sweepers pass down barren roads
The birds nest on the brick wall divider
Gun shots ring during the drive by outside
And the couple remain insiders

In a new land so far from home
A new language, friends and little money
Taking odd jobs, family left behind
Missing Quebec so sunny

Many years and generations later
The couple remain today
Still inside, still speaking French
But their grandkids visit on Sunday

A Little Bit

I'd like to see you naked
But just a little bit
Some lingerie and candles
Show just a little tit

It's getting hot and heavy
Show me just a little dick
Oh! I didn't realize
You had just a little bit

* Written upon request from my grandmother, my first
ever "dirty" poem

Little Bit

I'd like to see ya nuked
~~and~~ ~~oooooo~~
But just a little bit
Some lingerie and candles
Show just a little tit

It's getting hot and heavy
~~So pull out~~ your dick
Oh! I didn't realize
You had ~~oooo~~ a little bit
just

First Draft of A Little Bit

4

Me 2.0

The Aftermath

It's hard to grapple with the phrase "you can't cheat on someone you love," knowing I was cheated on my entire marriage essentially means it was loveless on his side. I was not loved or respected even though I loved and respected him. That's hard. I think in the early years of the relationship, the love between us was real and somewhere along the way he stopped. Sad after I defended him so vigorously through a lot of court shit. While I know his cheating has nothing to do with me, my self-esteem and confidence is shot. I feel ugly. I am scared to be romantic or sexual with other people. I'm nervous for someone to see me naked or know me intimately. I used to be a confident and comfortable (sometimes too comfortable) sexual being. My heart has been shattered by infidelity. I want to feel pretty again. I feel foolish and embarrassed, I don't even want to see my friends in person. It's hard to look at happy memories from our marriage. Should I still feel happy about them? Is it wrong?

I'm the One Who's Crying

If the other woman
Always cries herself to sleep
Was she the other woman
Or was the other woman me

Life Lately

Life Lately

Misery and sadness
And wallowing
Don't seem to mind me
Why can't peace
And happiness
And love ever seem to find me

Vitamins

Women are called meals or snacks but not me, I am never enough. Not to my ex-husband, not to the new men I date, not to anyone. There must always be a supplement, a second person to do whatever it is I can't.

October 4th Entry

Now I must talk about divine timing. In July I started having a feeling like something bad was going to happen, but I didn't know what. I thought it had something to do with his trial like he might go to jail. I decided to put the house up for sale and we accepted an offer within a week. I also got promoted in August. Then I found out he was cheating on me. Right before this, he took me to Tiffany to buy a necklace – the last time he did this we broke up. I knew seriously then something terrible was going to happen. I feel like if I didn't divorce him, I would be going against the universe or God or whatever this divine feeling was. I have never felt or experienced anything like it, but I must follow it and believe it is leading me somewhere better.

Favorites

I don't get to be anyone's favorite. My parent's favorite child is my sister. Grandma's favorite is a different cousin. My other grandparent's favorite is my mom. I wasn't even the favorite of my own ex-husband. It's depressing and while I know it to be true I hate to be reminded of it. I wish everyone would stop speaking of it as I'm learning to be my own favorite.

October 13th Entry

Sometimes when I feel happy and all of those good feelings come around, it makes me feel embarrassed. Like I'm soft, like I'm betraying my tough girl persona and it's all fake. When I'm depressed and woeful, it's draining and a waste of time. It makes me angry which is another feeling I don't want to feel all of the time. The anger makes me feel evil and cruel. I will just have to feel all of my emotions and deal with it. Not happy about it.

2024 Motivation Board Collage

The Aftermath, Months Later

I love life. It's warm out. I read, I paint, I watch anything I want on TV in my cute apartment. I do yoga. I cook and eat whatever I want. Work is busy but good. I'm not stressed. I do ballet and eat brownies. I have a crush. I write.

7|1

I love life. It's warm out.
I read, I paint, I watch
anything I want on my TV in
my cute apartment. Work is
busy but good. I do ballet and
eat brownies. I have a
crush. I write.

Mine All Mine

My love is so simple
I tell you about a movie
And you put it on your watch list

Alone

Of course I could do it all alone
But I don't want to

An Entry in Two Parts

Part 1

I'm manifesting that if I ever get back in a relationship again, I must be feminine. I want to be chased. I want a respectful, classy man. I want to be asked on a date, asked to be exclusive, and then have a nice proposal to get engaged. I want my man to be the man. I don't want to wear the pants. I want my man to be loyal, kind, hardworking, willing to take charge, good in bed, funny, and someone that will do the manly stuff like taking out the trash and maintaining my car. If I get married again, I don't want to get divorced. I want to travel and grow old together. I want us to love each other despite our flaws. Be honest and open. I want someone to respect me and take me seriously, someone who wants the same things as me.

Part 2

I am a misandrist. Men are stupid and disgusting and I am sadly attracted to them. There are always outliers, but I am speaking as a whole. I still want to marry a man and be in love despite this though. They don't respect you when you are vocal about your thoughts and feelings or when you are comfortable in your sexuality. When they see that your sexuality could benefit them though, they demand you have sex with them or at least send naked pictures. Go fuck yourself. Wars and conflict are built upon toxic masculinity. Everything good in life is a product of the divine feminine. I love women.

Geminis

Like a great wind you've swept me
Just as a gale bends grass in a plain
Am I dumfounded or just enamored
So carefree I've forgotten my name

There's but 2,000 miles between us
I, who lives so close to Boston
I'd walk it, fly it, dance it, or run it
Because my heart is drawn to Austin

Haiku 2

Fresh linens and sun
Windows are open so wide
Laying in my bed

Nobody

At night after work when it's time to relax
I sing songs from when I was young
I look beside me to join in the joy
Nobody is there for which to be sung

On the weekends I bake cookies and cakes
I stuff myself in front of the TV
I ask nobody if they want a bite
And nobody eats with me

I take care of house, I work, I relax
I have the life of which I've dreamed
Nobody's here to grow old with me
At my accomplishments, nobody beams

Nobody lives here with me
Nobody loves me, nobody cares
Nobody is my true companion
Nobody, with this life I could share

Into the Ether

All of my thoughts and all of my feelings I say out loud or write them down and for what? Who hears them, who is listening? Everything that comes out of my mouth, my heart, my soul it all floats into the ether.

But

If things can come out of the blue, can things come out of the ether? If I speak of happiness will I be guided to it? If I think of love will it find me? When I speak of all the good will it gravitate to me like I am the earth waiting to eat a fallen apple from a tree? Will it ever be me?